POMPEII

THE DAY A CITY WAS BURIED

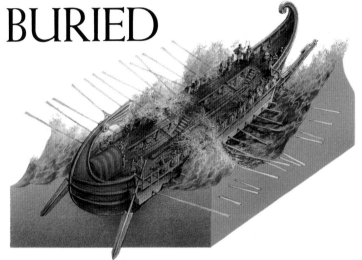

The admiral of the Roman fleet received a plea for help.

A busy street in Pompeii, the day before the eruption

Casts of victims of Vesuvius

The eruption of Vesuvius plunged the area into darkness, and whipped up the sea.

POMPEII

THE DAY A CITY WAS BURIED

Written by
MELANIE AND CHRISTOPHER RICE
Illustrated by
RICHARD BONSON

DORLING KINDERSLEY
LONDON • NEW YORK • MOSCOW • SYDNEY

A DORLING KINDERSLEY BOOK

Project Editor Francesca Baines
Art Editor Joanna Pocock
Senior Editor Scarlett O'Hara
Senior Art Editor Vicky Wharton
Senior Managing Editor Linda Martin
Senior Managing Art Editor Julia Harris
DTP Designer Almudena Díaz
Picture Research Catherine Edkins
Jacket Designer Mark Haygarth
Production Lisa Moss
Consultant Keith Lye

First published in 1998
by Dorling Kindersley Limited,
9 Henrietta Street, London WC2E 8PS

2 4 6 8 10 9 7 5 3 1

Copyright © 1998 Dorling Kindersley Ltd., London

Visit us on the World Wide Web at
http://www.dk.com

A CIP catalogue record for this book is available
from the British Library

ISBN 0 7513 5803 7

Reproduced by Colourscan, Singapore
Printed and bound by L.E.G.O., Italy

Additional illustrations by John Lawrence and Venice
Shone. Additional picture research by Lee Thomson.

Contents

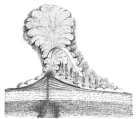

Pompeii:
A Window on the Past

POMPEII WAS AN unimportant Roman town in southern Italy, but it has a unique place in history. Buried for 1,700 years under a blanket of volcanic ash, it was rediscovered almost perfectly preserved. Since then, archaeologists and historians have been piecing together the lives of the people who lived there. This is their story.

Street scene in Pompeii before the eruption by Raffaele Gianetti (1832–1916).

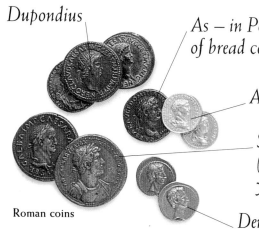

Dupondius

As – in Pompeii, a loaf of bread cost two asses.

Aureus

Sesterce – for 520 sesterces (each worth four asses) you could buy a mule.

Roman coins

Denarius

There were shrines
to the gods on
many shop walls.

THE ROMAN EMPIRE

POMPEII WAS ONLY A SMALL PART OF a great Roman civilization: the first Roman Emperor, Augustus, boasted on his deathbed that he had brought the "whole world under the rule of the Roman people". Over many centuries, Rome had grown from a cluster of trading settlements on the banks of the River Tiber into a great military and economic power, expanding its influence throughout the Mediterranean. Vast quantities of goods: gold, silver, priceless works of art, and slaves flowed into the capital, while towns like Pompeii, protected by the Roman army, were able to trade in peace.

City on the Tiber
Modern Rome, capital of Italy, is built on the ruins of the ancient city, once the capital of the Roman Empire. Spread out over seven hills, imperial Rome was by far the largest city in the ancient world with an estimated population of one million. The remains of shops, baths, theatres, temples and other public buildings can still be seen in the centre of Rome today.

THE STORY OF ROME

753 BC Rome founded
Rome took its name from its first ruler, Romulus, who according to legend, had been left to die by the River Tiber with his brother Remus. The babies were found and raised by a she-wolf.

Romulus and Remus are suckled by a wolf.

A debate in the Senate

510 BC The Roman Republic
The ruling king, Tarquinius, said to be a descendant of Romulus, was expelled from Rome as a tyrant. The city became an independent republic, governed by two consuls elected each year by a Senate (council) of nobles.

264 BC War with Carthage
A series of wars began with the North African power, Carthage, for control of the Mediterranean. Rome emerged triumphant in 146 BC when the famous general, Scipio, razed the city of Carthage to the ground.

A Roman war galley

80 BC Pompeii colonised
After a siege, the Romans took over Pompeii and moved settlers into the town.

Boudicca, the warrior queen

AD 43–61 Britain invaded
Britain became a Roman province as advancing armies put down revolts by tribes such as the Iceni, led by Queen Boudicca.

AD 62 Earthquake in Pompeii
Pompeii was at the centre of a severe earthquake, which also shook buildings in the nearby cities of Nuceria and Neapolis (Naples). Rebuilding began immediately.

AD 79 Eruption of Vesuvius
Pompeii and Herculaneum were buried under volcanic ash and almost forgotten.

Mount Vesuvius erupts.

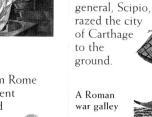

A barbarian on horseback

AD 286 The barbarian threat
Barbarians (tribes the Romans considered "uncivilized") threatened the northern and eastern frontiers. In an attempt to make governing easier, the Emperor Diocletian divided the Empire into East and West.

Emperor Constantine saw a vision of a flaming cross in the sky.

The Roman Empire AD 117

AT ITS HEIGHT the Roman Empire stretched from Spain in the west to Syria in the east, and from Britain in the north to Egypt in the south.

The symbol of the Republic
The defence of the Roman Empire depended on a well-trained and disciplined army. Troops carried standards that bore the letters *SPQR*, which stood for "The Senate and People of Rome".

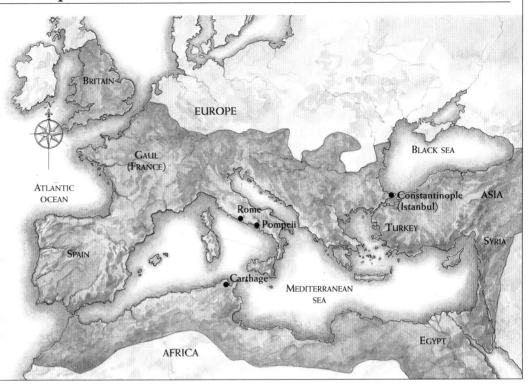

BRITAIN
EUROPE
GAUL (FRANCE)
BLACK SEA
ATLANTIC OCEAN
Constantinople (Istanbul)
ASIA
Rome
Pompeii
TURKEY
SYRIA
SPAIN
Carthage
MEDITERRANEAN SEA
EGYPT
AFRICA

73 BC Slave revolt
The Thracian gladiator Spartacus led a slave revolt in 73 BC. At one time, he camped in the crater of Mount Vesuvius. The rebellion was crushed two years later.

Spartacus leads the revolt

In this well-known cartoon, Asterix and Obelix the Gauls have fun thwarting their Roman rulers.

59–51 BC Conquest of Gaul
Under the rule of the powerful general Julius Caesar, the Romans occupied Gaul (France).

44 BC Julius Caesar murdered
Fearful that Caesar planned to overthrow the Republic and become king, a group of senators assassinated him.

The death of Caesar

31 BC Republic to Empire
Caesar's great-nephew Octavian ended a period of civil war by defeating Mark Antony at the Battle of Actium. He changed the Roman constitution and declared himself Emperor and sole ruler, under the name Augustus.

Augustus

AD 312 Christianity recognised
Constantine became ruler of the Western Empire after defeating his rival Maxentius in battle. He attributed his victory to the vision of a cross, which he believed was a sign from God. As a result Christianity was legalized.

AD 330 A new capital
Byzantium (now Istanbul) became the new capital of the Eastern Empire and was renamed Constantinople after the Emperor Constantine.

Constantinople (Istanbul)

Attila, leader of the Huns

AD 410 The sack of Rome
The barbarian leader Alaric entered Rome and sacked the city. Subsequent invasions by Goths, Vandals, Huns, and other tribes further weakened the Western Empire, and Rome itself fell into ruins.

AD 476 The last Emperor
The last Western emperor was deposed by Odoacer, a barbarian chief. The Eastern, Byzantine, Empire continued until 1453.

Barbarian spear and arrowheads

A MEDITERRANEAN TOWN

IN AD 79, POMPEII WAS A PROSPEROUS Mediterranean town situated on a broad plateau, 10 km (6 miles) south of Mount Vesuvius and overlooking the beautiful coastline of the Bay of Naples. A busy harbour had grown up at the mouth of the River Sarno, which flowed past the fortified walls of the town. Ships arrived here from Greece, Spain, Syria, and North Africa, unloading cargoes of mostly luxury goods, such as papyrus, glassware, pottery, precious jewels, dried fruits, and spices. These were exchanged for locally produced wine and cereals and an expensive fish paste called *garum*.

Rows of vines

Wine production
The only painting to depict Vesuvius before the eruption (above) was found on the wall of a house at Pompeii. It also shows Bacchus, the god of wine, protecting vines growing on the slopes of the volcano. Pompeian wine was in great demand – one farm stored up to 100,000 litres (22,000 gallons) to sell to local taverns as well as for export.

Pompeian grapes produced rough, strong wines.

MUREX SHELLS
The purple dye from murex shells was used to colour the emperor's robes.

UNDERWATER LIFE
The artist who created this mosaic, discovered in a house in Pompeii, had fun depicting the catches of local fishermen. At the centre of the picture, an octopus struggles with a lobster. Other fish in the picture include red mullet, squid, bass, eel, and even a spiky murex shell.

Fish sauce

HERBS, SPICES, and strong sauces were used to flavour food. In Pompeii, they were used in the popular sharp-flavoured, salty sauce called *garum*.

Celery

Roman flavourings

Herbs and spices

Recipe for garum
Finely chop a whole fish. Pound and stir, then leave to ferment in the sun. Season well with salt before straining into jars.

Mediterranean fish

When Rome was attacked by barbarians in the 5th century, Ravenna became the temporary capital of the Western Empire.

RICH VOLCANIC SOIL
Vesuvius is only one of many volcanoes around the Bay of Naples. Volcanic ash is full of nutrients, which have enriched the soil over the centuries, creating ideal pastures for sheep to graze.

Roman sheep statuette

WOOL TRADE
Wool was vital to Pompeii's economy. The fullers who made cloth and the merchants who sold it were among the richest citizens in Pompeii.

Rivers like the Tiber, the Arno, and the Po were important inland waterways used by traders to transport goods.

SEASIDE VILLAS
Retired generals and other wealthy Romans built luxurious holiday homes for themselves on the shores of the Bay of Naples. They were attracted by the mild winters, long, hot summers and peaceful surroundings.

The Romans built a road, called the Via Appia, from Rome to Brindisi to help them defend their territories in the south.

Today, Mount Etna is one of the world's largest active volcanoes. The Romans believed it was the forge of Vulcan, the god of fire.

ITALY
Italy lies in the centre of the Mediterranean Sea. The Italian peninsula is very mountainous: the Apennine range runs almost the entire length of the country from north to south. Pompeii is situated about 100 km (56 miles) south of Rome in a particularly fertile region known as Campania.

11

> "I'll show you where to find all sorts of men, good or bad or honest men or rascals."
>
> The playwright Plautus (254–184 BC) describing the forum in Rome.

THE PEOPLE OF POMPEII

WE KNOW MORE ABOUT THE PEOPLE OF Pompeii than almost any other ancient society because so much of what they left behind has been preserved – it has even been possible to make casts of their bodies! The characters below, based on real Pompeians, are imagined meeting in the forum.

A DISPUTE

Legal disputes between Pompeians were settled by a judge in the basilica (law court and stock exchange). The fuller (cloth maker), Vesonius, and the banker, Caecilius, might have gone there to sort out a quarrel, such as the repayment of a loan.

AT THE BARBER'S

Stalls selling all manner of goods and services were set up under the colonnades of the forum. The felt seller, Verecundus, may well have stopped for a shave and a haircut on his way to the *Eumachia* (cloth hall) to begin the day's trading.

STANDARD WEIGHTS
Market inspectors checked the weights used by traders.

THE FORUM

The main square of Pompeii, called the forum, was usually crowded with people: businessmen hurrying to their offices in the grain warehouses, politicians making speeches outside the basilica, priests making their way to the temple of Apollo, and stallholders bargaining with their customers in the arcades.

TEMPLE OF APOLLO
Apollo was the Roman god of the sun.

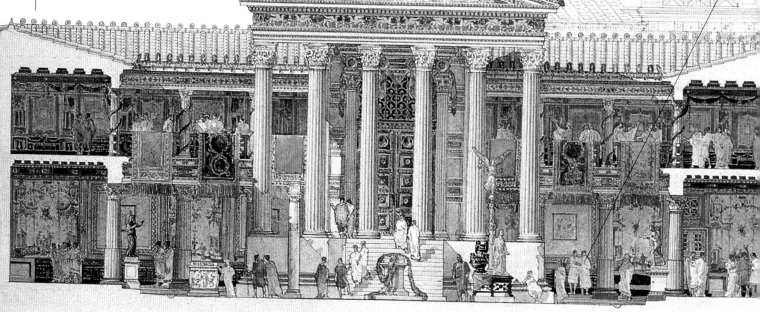

SHOPPING TRIP

Modestus, a baker in Pompeii, would have had many slaves working for him. One of them accompanied him to the *macellum* (food market) to buy jars of oil for his business.

ELECTION TIME

Citizens like the wine merchant Marcus Holconius and his friend were important figures in the political life of Pompeii. The sign painter Aemilius Celer would have been hired to write political slogans on the walls of the forum.

Graffiti

GRAFFITI covered many walls in Pompeii. The messages tell us about the feelings and opinions of ordinary people.

Vote for me!
This wall, on a main street, was covered with notices advertising goods for sale and gladiatorial shows as well as election propaganda.

POETRY PLEASE

Poetry recitals were a popular entertainment in Roman times. Local poets would stand outside the Temple of Jupiter and recite their latest verses to people who passed through the forum.

OFFICE SPACE
The grain warehouses had offices on their upper floors.

WORKS OF ART
Only the base of this statue was found, but we know it was of a horse because it is shown in the panel of the forum in Caecilius' house (see page 19).

TEMPLE OF JUPITER
Jupiter, chief of all the gods, had command over the heavens.

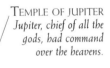

Birth rituals
A new-born baby would be placed at the feet of its father. If the baby was a boy and was healthy, his father would pick him up and hold him in his arms. A girl would be handed straight to the nurse.

Bulla
About a week after the birth of a male child, a gold amulet, known as a *bulla*, was placed around the baby's neck to signify that he was born free and not a slave.

GROWING UP IN POMPEII

GROWING UP AS A ROMAN CITIZEN WAS a serious business. Children were usually educated at home, either by a parent or a slave tutor. They learned their lessons by heart, and there were beatings for lazy pupils! Everyone learned to read and write – even slaves. Boys studied Greek, speech making, and law, as well as sports and military skills. Girls were taught how to run the household, while some slaves were instructed in arithmetic so that they could serve the family as stewards or accountants.

FATHERS AND SONS
In most households, fathers took the lead in bringing up their sons. The boy in this relief (left) is reciting a lesson to his father, who listens attentively. Children were encouraged to behave like adults, but there was also time for play – this boy is also shown riding his donkey chariot.

A BOY'S LIFE
This marble relief on a sarcophagus (tomb) shows episodes from a boy's childhood.

GROWING UP FAST
Roman children grew up quickly. When a boy reached the age of 15 or 16, a coming-of-age party would be held in his honour. The young man would leave his *bulla* and child's toga on the household *lararium* (shrine) as an offering to the gods, before proceeding to the forum with his father and friends to make a sacrifice.

YOUNG ADULTS
As can be seen in this street scene, imagined by the 19th-century painter Sir Lawrence Alma-Tadema, Roman children were treated like adults.

Stylus, used
to write on wax

Wax tablet

YOUNG WOMEN

Girls were brought up by their mothers at home, where they learned weaving and other domestic skills. They were considered grown-up by the age of 14, when marriages were arranged for them by their parents.

The household shrine

EVERY HOME had its own shrine, or *lararium*, dedicated to the household gods. Prayers were offered here daily by members of the family.

Painting from a household shrine

Genius

Lar

Spirits of protection and prosperity
The *genius* (protector of the household) is flanked by two *lares* (guardian spirits). The snake symbolizes abundance, or plenty.

Bees
Romans thought bees were the gods' messengers and brought good luck.

JUST MARRIED

On her wedding day, the bride wore her hair braided, in keeping with an old tradition. After the ceremony, the couple clasped hands to show that they were now man and wife, before leading a torchlight procession to the groom's home. As they passed, friends and relatives shouted *"feliciter"*, meaning good luck.

NUTS!
For good luck, the bride and groom would scatter walnuts among the crowd.

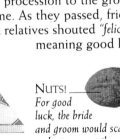

GODDESS OF LOVE
This statue was found in the house of a rich woman of Pompeii named Julia Felix.

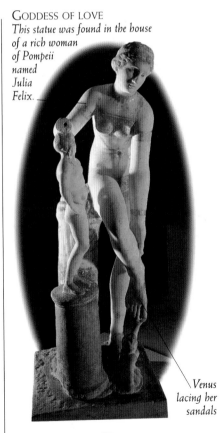

Venus lacing her sandals

The goddess of Pompeii
The Romans worshipped many different gods, but Venus, goddess of love, was the favourite of people in Pompeii. Statues and paintings of her have been discovered in houses, shops, and business premises.

GRAVE MATTERS

Roman health care was very basic – only about 50 per cent of children reached puberty. On this tombstone, ten-year-old Avita is remembered with her books and pet dog.

FACT file

• The Romans were very superstitious and chose the date for a wedding carefully. Months to be avoided included May, when the dead were remembered, and March, which was dedicated to Mars, god of War.

• It was the custom to place a coin in the mouth of a dead person to pay Charon the ferryman, who (the Romans believed) transported souls to the land of the dead.

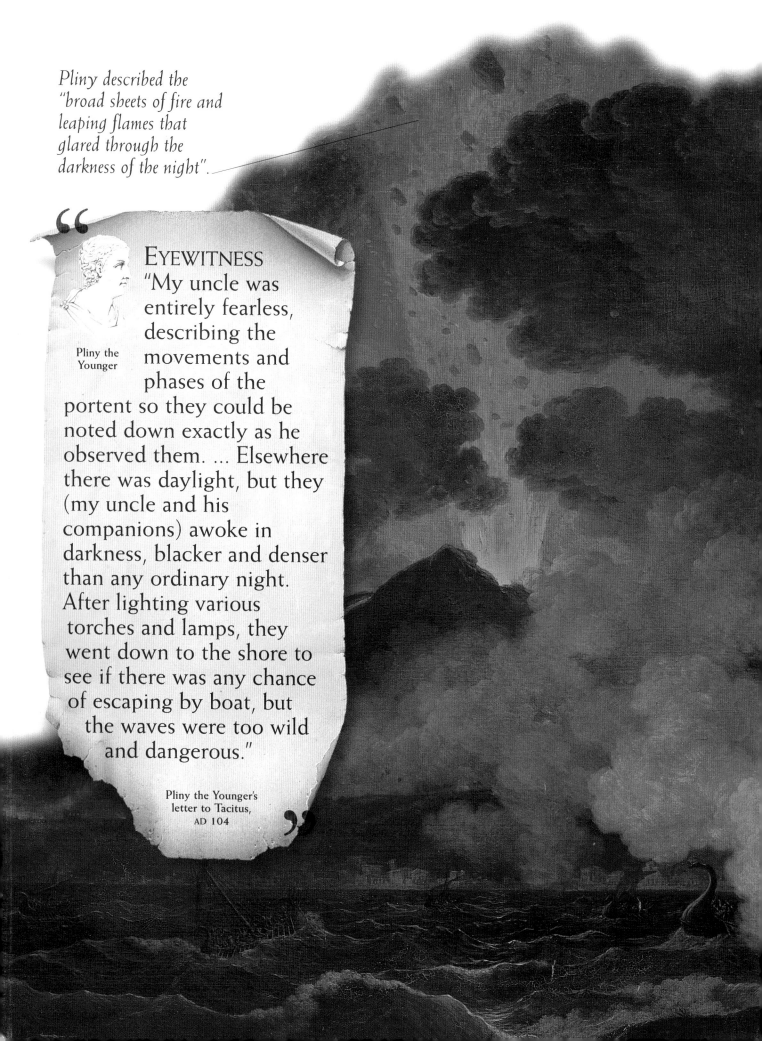

Pliny described the "broad sheets of fire and leaping flames that glared through the darkness of the night".

EYEWITNESS

"My uncle was entirely fearless, describing the movements and phases of the portent so they could be noted down exactly as he observed them. ... Elsewhere there was daylight, but they (my uncle and his companions) awoke in darkness, blacker and denser than any ordinary night. After lighting various torches and lamps, they went down to the shore to see if there was any chance of escaping by boat, but the waves were too wild and dangerous."

Pliny the Younger

Pliny the Younger's letter to Tacitus, AD 104

Eruption!

ON 24 AUGUST AD 79, tragedy struck Pompeii when Mount Vesuvius erupted. Pliny the Younger was an eyewitness to the events. He spoke to survivors and later wrote an account of his uncle's voyage into the disaster area.

A painting called *The Death of Pliny* by Pierre-Henri de Valenciennes, 1813

But even as they watched, the cloud began to drift slowly towards the town, the sky darkened, and flakes of white ash and pumice began to fall. People panicked. Some ran home to collect their belongings, others fled the town straight away, groping in the darkness as their hair and mouths were burnt by ash, and gasping for breath as they stumbled on the pumice stones littering the streets.

The debris rained down and all the roads were blocked. Houses started to collapse under the weight of volcanic ash and pumice. Poisonous gases seeped under the doors of houses, and people now fought to get out, even using axes to break down walls, struggling until the suffocating gases overcame them. Mothers and fathers covered the faces of their children, but by morning, few of those who had stayed behind were left alive.

EXPLOSION!
At around 1.00 pm, Vesuvius expelled a huge column of gas, pumice, and ash that rose to a height of 27 km (17 miles).

WALLS SHAKE
Builders, repairing the damage to the theatre caused by the earthquake of AD 62, ran for their lives as the scaffolding around them collapsed.

STAGE FRIGHT
The actors were so frightened that they didn't care how strange they looked running off in their costumes.

PRAYING FOR MERCY
For the priests of Isis, the priority was to save the statuettes and offerings of gold and silver in the temple. They collected them in linen sacks to take with them, but first they may have offered a hasty sacrifice to ask the goddess for protection.

FACT file
• Experts believe the population of Pompeii was 20,000. So far, only 2,000 bodies have been found, which suggests that many people managed to flee the town.

• Today, the area around Vesuvius is much more densely populated than in AD 79. If there was an eruption of the same scale now, hundreds of thousands of people might be killed.

NUMB WITH FEAR
Panic affects people in different ways. Dion's fellow actors begged him to leave the theatre, but he was too frightened to move and didn't even seem to hear what they were saying. In the end, they ran away, leaving Dion to his fate.

THE MOUNTAIN EXPLODES

THE SLAVES OF THE PRIESTS OF ISIS were serving a midday meal of bread, wine, chicken, fish, and eggs, when a deafening explosion shook the temple walls. Egg cups, plates, wine jugs, and glass bowls crashed to the floor as the terrified men ran out into the crowded street. Everyone stared at Vesuvius and at the plume of dense, black smoke rising from the summit.

Ghosts of Pompeii
This haunting portrait was found in a house in Pompeii. We don't know the identity of the young couple, although several names have been suggested by archaeologists. Whoever they were, they may have witnessed the dramatic events of 24 August.

LOOK OUT!
Tiles and bricks fell as the splendid buildings shook.

WARNING!
Farmers living on the slopes of Vesuvius warned of unusual activity on the mountain, but their words were ignored.

MONEY FIRST
Some people were less terrified than others. These shoppers were determined to get their change from the stallholder first!

GREAT ESCAPE
We know that Caecilius' son, Quintus, escaped to England. Perhaps Caecilius gave Quintus his horse before hurrying home on foot to join his wife.

THE COLLAPSE OF THE FORUM
The forum was the commercial and religious centre of Pompeii and a popular meeting place. Even on a festival day it would have been crowded with politicians, businessmen, and stallholders. Their first thought would have been to run away from the crumbling buildings.

PANIC IN THE STREETS
Despite the warning signs, the suddenness of the explosion must have caused havoc in the narrow streets as shoppers ran off in different directions, colliding with each other in the rush to escape.

IGNORING THE SIGNS

FOR FOUR DAYS BEFORE VESUVIUS erupted, there were earth tremors and rumblings deep underground. In Pompeii, doors creaked in their frames, hanging-lamps swung from side to side, and glasses clinked on shelves. But although the warning signs were there, most people ignored them, probably because it had happened before, not once but many times. In fact, there were tremors almost every year. What people didn't realize was that this time the mountain was about to explode.

Vulcan, god of fire
The Latin word for volcano, *vulcanus*, takes its name from the blacksmith Vulcan, the Roman god of fire. By coincidence, the festival of Vulcan would have been celebrated on 23 August, the day before the eruption.

CHILDREN'S GAMES
These children are playing jacks with knucklebones — the small, square bones from a sheep's foot.

EARLY WARNING
Children often played in the streets of Pompeii. These children were probably so busy with their game that they didn't notice when the water stopped flowing from the public fountain.

MARBLES
Pompeian children also played with marbles made of pottery, glass, or even nuts.

Pottery marbles

Glass marbles

STREET LIFE
There were no proper sewers in Pompeii and few drains. Rotting vegetables, butcher's offal, and other rubbish was dumped in the street to be washed away by the rain. In the hot, dry summers, the stench must have been unbearable.

VERECUNDUS THE FELT SELLER
Verecundus took a delivery of felt just before the eruption, little knowing that it would never be needed.

SIXTH SENSE
Flocks of seagulls flew away from the town — another indication of what was to come.

LIVING CONDITIONS

Most Pompeians lived in cramped conditions – usually a one- or two-roomed apartment above a shop. These homes would have lacked even basic amenities like a kitchen stove or running water. People who wanted a hot dinner could buy a takeaway from the local food shop (*thermopolium*). Fresh water had to be fetched from public fountains on street corners.

TRAPPED BIRDS
Pet birds would have fluttered nervously in their cages, sensing the approaching danger.

The earthquake of AD 62

ONLY 17 YEARS BEFORE VESUVIUS ERUPTED, Pompeii was severely damaged by a major earthquake. The banker Caecilius narrowly escaped with his life as the houses around him collapsed. Many buildings still lay in ruins or were under repair in AD 79.

Gratitude
Caecilius was so grateful to the gods for saving his life that he ordered a stone carving for his household shrine showing the swaying buildings. He did not realize that the earthquake was a warning.

Measuring earthquakes
Today the severity of an earthquake is measured on the Mercalli scale (from I-XII). The damage to these buildings (right) in the San Francisco earthquake of 1989 (level VIII) would probably have been similar to that in Pompeii.

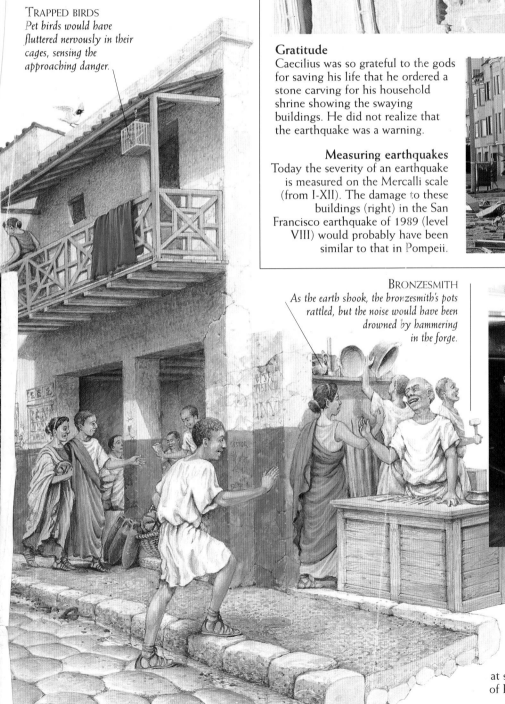

BRONZESMITH
As the earth shook, the bronzesmith's pots rattled, but the noise would have been drowned by hammering in the forge.

Earthquake drill
In Japan, there are 67 active volcanoes and hundreds of earthquakes every year. Most are barely noticeable, but a few cause buildings to sway and send objects crashing to the floor. Japanese children practise earthquake drill at school so that – unlike the children of Pompeii – they know what to do as soon as the tremors begin.

Taking flight

Parts of Julia Felix's house had been damaged by earlier earth tremors, so she knew the danger of staying indoors. She must have left straight away with her maid, taking just a few treasured possessions.

TREASURES ABANDONED
In her haste to escape, Julia Felix had to leave many precious objects behind, including a beautiful statue of Venus.

PLAYING UNTIL THE END
Some gladiators died leaving their trumpets at their feet. Presumably they had been playing their instruments until they were overcome by the fumes.

NO CARES

At the time of the eruption Pompeii was celebrating the Festival of the Divine Augustus. It was a public holiday so the taverns in Pompeii would have been busy. The customers here were enjoying themselves so much that they ignored everything that was going on outside.

Last stand

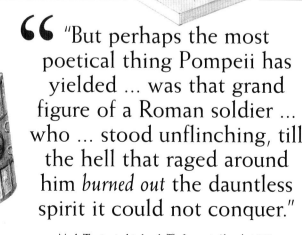

Standing firm
The body of a Roman legionary was found near the town gate where he had been standing guard. For a Roman soldier to run away in the face of danger would have been unthinkable. Even if he had escaped, the punishment for deserting his post and bringing shame to the legion would have been death.

ON DUTY
The legionary was wearing a full set of armour when he died.

66 "But perhaps the most poetical thing Pompeii has yielded ... was that grand figure of a Roman soldier ... who ... stood unflinching, till the hell that raged around him *burned out* the dauntless spirit it could not conquer."

Mark Twain, in his book *The Innocents Abroad*, 1875.

CONGESTION

The houses and apartments in Pompeii were crammed with families and tenants renting every available room. Anyone trying to escape would have found it difficult – there were no fire escapes or emergency exits in the buildings, and many of the heavy outer doors were barred to keep out thieves. The darkness must have added to the confusion.

A dog's death

Left to die

Rufus, the guard dog belonging to Vesonius the fuller (cloth maker), was found chained up in the atrium of his house. As ash and pumice rained down through the hole in the roof, the poor animal struggled frantically with his chain and bronze collar, but was unable to break free.

FORGOTTEN IN THE CHAOS
Some animals and pets were left behind by their owners.

TRAPPED!
The skeletons of men forgotten in the panic were later found in the punishment cells.

TOO LATE
Outside the barracks, slaves were loading up a donkey but, if they were planning to escape, they did not get away in time.

DROP EVERYTHING
These gladiators left their swords and helmets behind, realizing they would only get in the way.

RUN FOR YOUR LIFE
The people in the bakery fled quickly, stopping only to gather up the day's takings.

NO WAY OUT

Some gladiators, like the handsome Crescens, decided to stay put and brave it out. Perhaps he wanted to reassure the wealthy lady who was visiting the barracks at the time. Unfortunately, the gladiators knew nothing about the poisonous gases from volcanoes; they would have been wiser to leave.

ESCAPE FROM THE BAKERY

Modestus was baking bread in his oven when Vesuvius erupted – the charred remains of 81 loaves were discovered much later. We can only guess what happened to Modestus afterwards. There were no animal bones found near the flour mill, so he may have ridden away on his donkey.

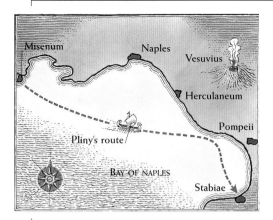

THE FINAL HOURS

THE UNUSUAL BLACK CLOUD HANGING over Vesuvius attracted the attention of the naturalist Pliny the Elder, who lived in nearby Misenum. He decided to investigate and ordered a boat to be made ready. As he was leaving, he received a plea for help from Rectina, a friend who lived at the foot of Vesuvius. His trip now became a rescue mission. It was only 26 km (16 miles) to Pompeii and with a strong wind Pliny made good time, but rough seas made it impossible to land. Instead he sailed on to Stabiae, a decision that was to cost him his life.

An ill wind
A northwesterly wind helped Pliny's ship speed across the Bay of Naples to the shore at the foot of Vesuvius. Later, the same wind would blow the deathly cloud of ash towards Stabiae.

S.O.S.
A messenger brought a note begging for Pliny's help.

EYEWITNESS
"For a moment my uncle considered turning back, but when the helmsman advised this he refused, quoting the Roman proverb *fortes fortuna invat* (fortune favours the brave)."

Letter from Pliny the Younger, AD 104

A CALL FOR HELP
Pliny's nephew, Pliny the Younger, was staying at Misenum when the messenger arrived. He decided to stay behind and later wrote two letters to the historian Tacitus, describing what had happened. These letters provide us with a first-hand account of the eruption.

DRENCHED
Water flooded the galleys where the slaves were rowing.

DANGER ZONE
Pliny was commander of the naval base at Misenum and ordered the fleet to put to sea. Pliny's ship made fast progress but, as it entered the danger zone, the prow took a battering from the floating pumice, broken ship's masts, and other debris whipped up by the raging sea.

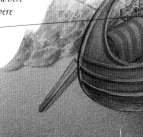

A hail of rock

Exploding lava

The eruption of AD 79 was an explosion of gas and thick lava. As it met the air, the lava blasted into tiny pieces, creating ash, dust, pumice (small, light stones filled with bubbles of air), and large, heavy chunks called volcanic bombs.

Volcanic dust

Volcanic ash

Pumice stones

DARKNESS
Throughout 25 August, the clouds of ash were so thick they obscured all daylight.

DRIVEN BACK
Furious winds blew boats back onto the beach, making it impossible to escape by sea.

SHELTER
Finding themselves trapped, people took refuge in boat chambers built into the harbour wall.

BATTERED
People covered their heads with pillows to protect them from the raining pumice.

TRAPPED

Through the darkness of the volcanic cloud Pliny could make out the flickering lights of a port and could even hear cries for help from the beach. However, the shore was blocked by debris from the mountain, and he could not land. Disappointed, he decided to sail on to Stabiae, where he spent the night with his friend Pomponianus.

LAST HOURS

When Pliny woke the next morning, the house was shaking and ash had piled up against the door. Slaves helped him down to the beach for safety, but he died, probably overcome by poisonous fumes.

The Lost City

AFTER THE ERUPTION OF AD 79, Pompeii was buried and forgotten. Although local people talked of a "city" that had once existed in the area, farmers grazed their sheep and grew crops on the land. From time to time people discovered pieces of marble with Latin inscriptions, but it was not until the 18th century that archaeologists finally began excavating Pompeii.

Photograph of excavations at Pompeii in the 1890s.

"Nothing lasts for ever. Though the sun shines gold, it must sink into the sea. The moon has also disappeared, which but now so brightly gleamed. So if the loved one rages, hold fast, this storm will soon yield to the gentle zephyr."

Graffiti from a wall in Pompeii

Teams of workers carried away rocks and earth in straw baskets.

These figures were found in the Garden of the Fugitives (a cemetery just outside the town).

The casts of the bodies of a mother and child

This villa became known as The House of the Silver Wedding because it was discovered in 1893, the 25th wedding anniversary of the King and Queen of Italy.

Supervisors made sure no one stole any of the finds.

THE DISCOVERY

THE QUEST FOR THE LOST CITIES OF Vesuvius began almost by chance when, in 1709, a peasant called Resina found several slabs of marble while digging a well. In the scramble for buried treasure that followed, no one thought about conservation, and many items of value were destroyed or lost. It was not until 1864, when Giuseppe Fiorelli was put in charge of excavations, that proper scientific records were kept of the site.

First tourists
During the 18th century, Pompeii became one of Europe's most popular tourist attractions. The painter Jacob Hackert visited the site in 1799. His picture shows the colonnaded courtyard of the gladiators' barracks and the theatre.

Treasure chest

Finds at Pompeii range from jewellery to loaves of bread, but every item is a valuable clue to Roman life. These objects are now in museums so that visitors from all over the world can marvel at them.

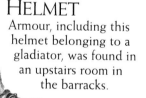

Volcanic gases turned this loaf to charcoal (a process known as carbonization). They even preserved the baker's stamp.

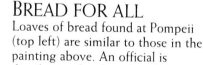

HELMET
Armour, including this helmet belonging to a gladiator, was found in an upstairs room in the barracks.

BREAD FOR ALL
Loaves of bread found at Pompeii (top left) are similar to those in the painting above. An official is distributing free bread to the townspeople, possibly on a public holiday. At least ten different types of bread were on sale in Pompeii and even a kind of dog biscuit.

BEWARE OF THE DOG
This mosaic, outside a house in Pompeii, warned visitors to beware of the dog (*cave canem*). The House of the Faun had a mosaic "welcome" sign in its doorway.

SNAKE CHARM
This twisted gold snake armband was one of a pair found at Pompeii. The snake was also a popular motif for rings and bracelets.

Herculaneum

AT FIRST, it was thought that the people of Herculaneum had escaped the effects of the volcano. But, in 1982, human skeletons were discovered on the beach, and then hundreds more were found huddled in boathouses on the seafront, where they had taken refuge.

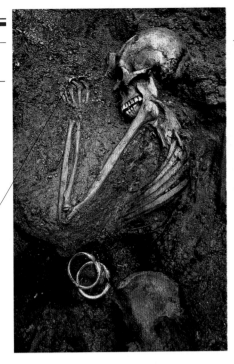

The skeleton still wore two beautiful gold rings.

FIORELLI AT WORK
Giuseppe Fiorelli (shown here supervising excavations) divided Pompeii into nine regions, and he numbered the blocks of houses and house entrances. When an object was removed from the site, he could record exactly where it was found.

The site today
Archaeologists have been able to excavate only a small part of Herculaneum because it lies 20 m (65 ft) below the new town of Resina.

Ring lady
One of the skeletons found in a boathouse was named the "Ring Lady" by archaeologists because of the gold jewellery found with her body.

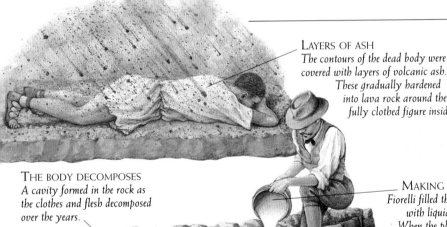

LAYERS OF ASH
The contours of the dead body were covered with layers of volcanic ash. These gradually hardened into lava rock around the fully clothed figure inside.

THE BODY DECOMPOSES
A cavity formed in the rock as the clothes and flesh decomposed over the years.

MAKING A CAST
Fiorelli filled the cavity with liquid plaster. When the plaster set, the lava was chipped away to reveal a perfect cast.

FACT file

• In 1943, during the Second World War, buildings were damaged when an Allied air raid dropped 162 bombs on Pompeii by mistake.

• 132 writing tablets were found in the house of Caecilius the banker. These revealed the business accounts of many wealthy Pompeians.

• In 1990, thieves stole over 250 artefacts from a storeroom in Herculaneum, including the jewels of the "Ring Lady".

BROUGHT TO LIFE
Fiorelli is best known for his ingenious method of reconstructing people, animals, and objects that had decomposed over the years. The technique even enabled him to recreate details such as hair, clothes, and facial expressions.

MODERN TECHNIQUES
Since 1984, epoxy resins (more resistant to wear and tear) have been used to make casts instead of plaster.

CAUSE OF DEATH
This woman is lying as if in sleep, her head cradled on one arm. She had pulled her tunic up over her face to keep the suffocating fumes from her nose and mouth.

REVISITING THE PAST

ARCHAEOLOGISTS, LIKE GOOD DETECTIVES, sift carefully through the remains of an ancient site looking for evidence of how people lived in the past. These pages show how, in Pompeii, they discovered a bar with the original counter, storage jars, and even a household shrine. From these finds, they could imagine how people ate, drank, and socialised 1,900 years ago.

Painstaking work
Archaeologists continue to work at the site today. Each find is measured and photographed to record its exact position. The soil is removed using small trowels or brushes so that nothing is damaged.

THE BAR TODAY
Over 200 buildings in Pompeii served food and drink. These ranged from inns with rooms to let to simple bars with a counter facing the street. The main features of the bar with the *lararium* (shrine) look much as they would have done around 2,000 years ago.

AMPHORAE
Wine was stored in pottery jars, called amphorae *but sold in smaller measures, called* carafes *or* cucumae.

The Italian archaeologist Spinazzola inspecting the Via dell'Abbondanza.

PROTECTION
Shops, as well as houses, were protected by lares (spirits).

THE EXCAVATION
Spinazzola discovered the bar with the *lararium* while excavating the main shopping street, which he later called *Via dell'Abbondanza* (Street of Abundance). Spinazzola worked on the site from 1910 to 1924.

THE COUNTER
Snacks, hot vegetable stews, and wine were served from earthenware jars sunk into the counter.

THE DAY'S TAKINGS
The bar must have been busy on the day of the eruption because 683 sesterces (coins) were found in a jar on the counter.

Made in Pompeii

ARCHAEOLOGISTS WORKING IN POMPEII have turned up vast quantities of red earthenware pottery, evidence that this was an important local industry. Pompeian wine *amphorae* stamped with the name of the Eumachii family have been found as far away as southern France.

Cooking pot on trivet

Earthenware jar set in counter

Piping hot
This diagram shows how the stone counter of the bar insulated the jar, keeping food and drink hot for long periods.

Some jugs were highly decorative.

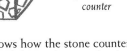

Rooster jug

Water jug

THE BAR IN AD 79

In Roman times, customers in this bar could chose from a variety of wines – Falernian, "the drink of the emperors" was four times more expensive than the local wine *Pompeiiana*. Snacks included nuts, olives, bread, cheese, and onions.

SERVING
We know that women as well as men served behind the counter – most were slaves.

ROWDY CROWD
Bars were lively places. Wall paintings show customers gambling, brawling, and being thrown out drunk.

Pompeii under threat
Pollution, vandalism, theft, and neglect caused by lack of funding are some of the problems facing the site administrators today. Another major concern is how to cater for the two million visitors who come to Pompeii each year.

WELL SEALED
This type of amphora was sealed with a cork disc fixed with cement.

POMPEII REVEALED

POMPEII COVERED AN AREA OF ABOUT 60 hectares (145 acres). The streets were laid out in a grid pattern and surrounded by a massive fortified wall containing 8 gates and 11 watchtowers. Not all the destruction in Pompeii was caused by the volcano. Finds such as wooden scaffolding and piles of lime indicated that the earthquake 17 years earlier had also caused extensive damage and that repairs were underway.

Pompeii today
Even after 200 years of excavation, archaeologists have uncovered only about 60 per cent of Pompeii. But the expense of preserving the 1,500 buildings has meant that there is little money left over for exploring new areas.

A RECONSTRUCTION
This bird's-eye view of Pompeii in AD 79 shows many of the sites mentioned in this book. Surprisingly few streets were named, so strangers to the town would have had to ask locals for directions.

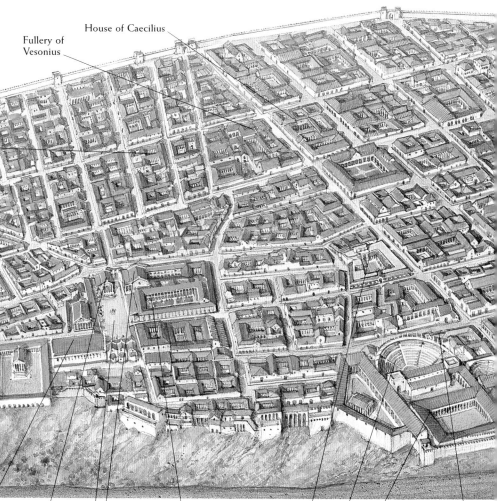

House of Caecilius

Fullery of Vesonius

House of the Faun

Bakery of Modestus

THE HARBOUR GATE
In AD 79, Pompeii was 500 m (½ mile) from the sea. Volcanic debris filled in the bay, and it is now 2 km (1 ¼ miles) inland.

Basilica (law court-and-stock exchange)

Temple of Jupiter

Forum

Macellum (food market)

THE EUMACHIA
Wool traders conducted their business in this magnificent building, endowed by the wealthy widow Eumachia and her son.

Stabian Baths

Theatre

Gladiators' barracks

TEMPLE OF ISIS
Sacrifices were offered daily to the Egyptian goddess Isis, popular with Pompeians.

IN THE BALANCE
Bronze scales like these were found in Pompeii. They were used for weighing produce in shops and in the *macellum* (food market).

LADY'S MIRROR
A superb mirror was among 118 precious silver objects found in a chest in the House of Menander. This palatial villa was named after a painting of the playwright Menander on one of the walls.

Silver mirror decorated with the head of a woman.

SHOPS
Verecundus' felt shop was on Pompeii's main street, now known as the Via dell'Abbondanza.

EGGS
A plate of petrified (fossilized) eggs, found in the Temple of Isis, was part of the priests' last meal.

CAECILIUS
This bronze bust is thought to be of Lucius Caecilius Felix, the father of Caecilius the banker. He grew rich dealing in slaves, cloth, and timber.

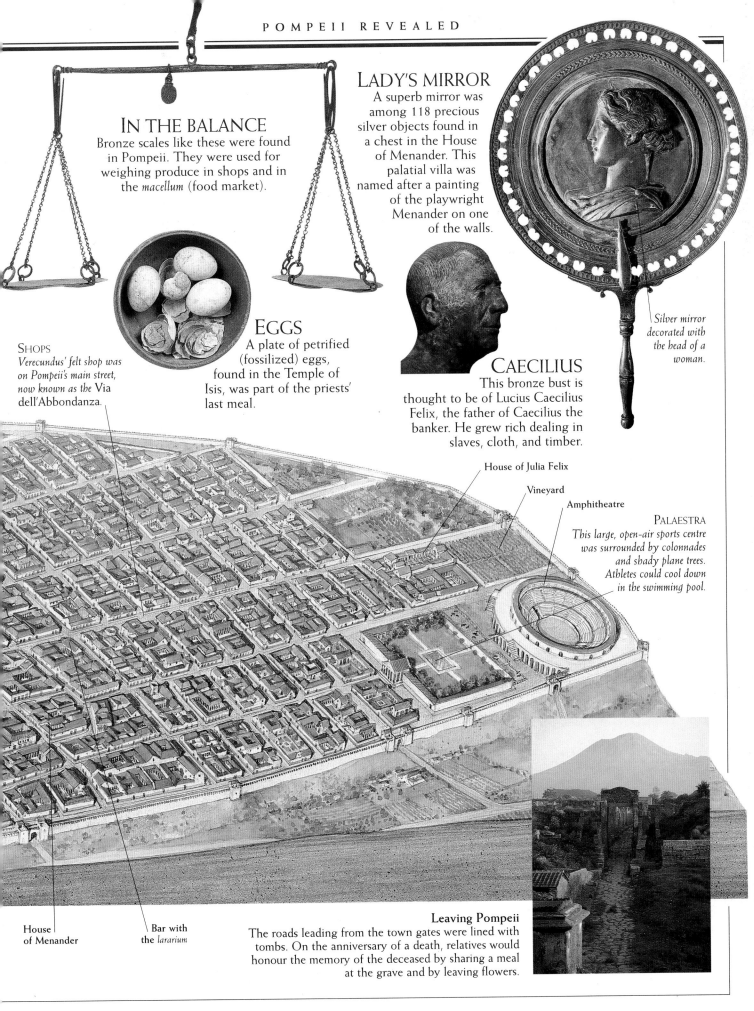

House of Julia Felix

Vineyard

Amphitheatre

PALAESTRA
This large, open-air sports centre was surrounded by colonnades and shady plane trees. Athletes could cool down in the swimming pool.

House of Menander

Bar with the *lararium*

Leaving Pompeii
The roads leading from the town gates were lined with tombs. On the anniversary of a death, relatives would honour the memory of the deceased by sharing a meal at the grave and by leaving flowers.

Everyday Life in Pompeii

THE PEOPLE OF POMPEII left behind not only their homes, personal possesions, and everyday objects, but paintings, mosaics, wall posters, and graffiti. By studying this evidence, historians can learn about daily life in a Roman town: what people ate, what kind of work they did, and the things that interested them. Just like people today, Pompeians fell in and out of love, squabbled, argued, and told jokes. Some children even wrote rude remarks about their teachers!

Squid

Carbonized figs

Hot ash and gas from the eruption turned this bowl of figs to charcoal.

Fresh figs

Figs grow well in the dry, stony soil around Pompeii.

Mosaic from Pompeii of a kitchen slave

A platter of figs

Fresh fish from the Mediterranean

"When the crops grow again and these deserts flower, will future generations believe that here, beneath their feet, lie cities and people?"

Verse by the poet Statius, written a few years after the eruption.

Bronze statue of a faun

A ROMAN TOWN HOUSE

WE DON'T ACTUALLY KNOW WHO LIVED in the House of the Faun, but we can imagine it was someone like the wealthy wine merchant Marcus Holconius and his family. Their day would have begun at dawn with a breakfast of bread, honey, and olives. Then, while Marcus received his clients in the atrium before leaving for the forum, his wife, would give the household slaves their orders for the day.

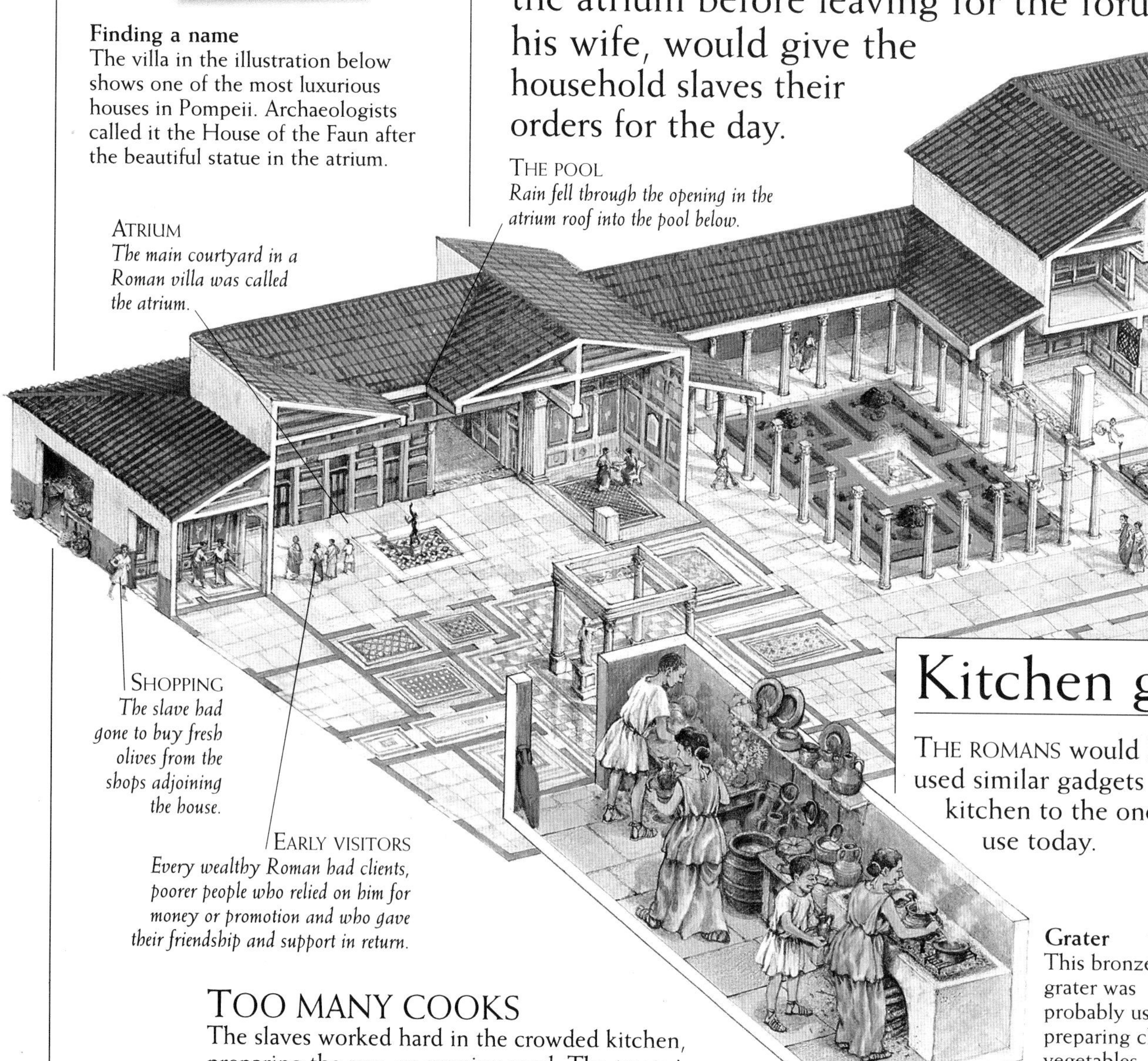

Finding a name
The villa in the illustration below shows one of the most luxurious houses in Pompeii. Archaeologists called it the House of the Faun after the beautiful statue in the atrium.

THE POOL
Rain fell through the opening in the atrium roof into the pool below.

ATRIUM
The main courtyard in a Roman villa was called the atrium.

SHOPPING
The slave had gone to buy fresh olives from the shops adjoining the house.

EARLY VISITORS
Every wealthy Roman had clients, poorer people who relied on him for money or promotion and who gave their friendship and support in return.

TOO MANY COOKS
The slaves worked hard in the crowded kitchen, preparing the *cena*, or evening meal. The treats in store included dormice in honey sprinkled with poppy seeds, spicy sausages, and thrushes rolled in flour and stuffed with nuts and raisins.

Kitchen gadgets

THE ROMANS would have used similar gadgets in the kitchen to the ones we use today.

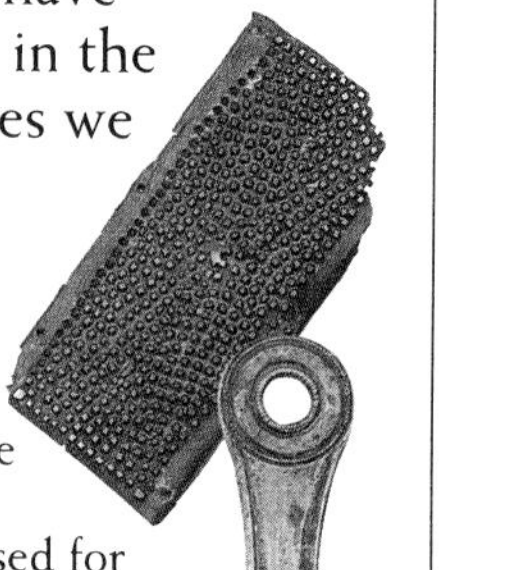

Grater
This bronze grater was probably used for preparing cheese and vegetables.

Strainer
This strainer was used to drain boiled or stewed food and to separate the juice from fruit.

FUN AND GAMES
Marcus' son and daughter would have played with the slave children under the watchful eye of their tutor.

SIESTA
Summer afternoons were hot. Marcus went to the baths, while his wife and children took a siesta (a short sleep). The only creatures with any energy were the lizards that came out to bask in the sun.

GARDENS
The Romans loved gardens with ponds and fountains, neatly trimmed bushes, and shady colonnades. They also liked scented flowers like roses, violets, and oleander.

Exquisite decoration
This brilliantly coloured mosaic was part of the floor decoration in the House of the Faun. It depicts crocodiles, hippos, and other exotic creatures found in the River Nile – the Pompeians were fascinated by the stories they heard about Egypt.

IN THE GARDEN
Slaves were not allowed to marry, but no one could stop them falling in love. This slave slipped out of the house to meet his girlfriend in the garden.

EATING HABITS
Romans reclined on couches and ate with their fingers.

COVERS
Slaves would have covered the couches with clean linen to prevent stains.

DINNER TIME
Dinner began at 4 pm and Marcus, his wife, and their friends would still have been eating at 8 pm. The meal had more than a dozen courses but, as portions were small, they didn't feel too full.

DRINKS
This slave has brought a local wine called Pompeiianum. Wine was always diluted with water and sometimes flavoured with honey and pepper.

RULES OF BEHAVIOUR
"Don't make eyes at another man's wife. Don't be coarse in your conversation. Don't get angry or use offensive language- if you can't control yourself, go home."

Written on the wall of a Pompeian dining room

THE PUBLIC BATHS

ROMAN BATHS WERE NOISY PLACES. THE WRITER SENECA, who lived above one, complained about people singing in the bath at the tops of their voices and shouting as they splashed about in the water. Pompeians, like other Romans, came to the baths to relax and unwind after a long morning's work. Apart from washing and bathing, they could gossip with friends, argue about politics, do business deals, play games, or take exercise. And, if they worked up an appetite, they could buy refreshments from vendors selling cakes, hot sausages, and drinks.

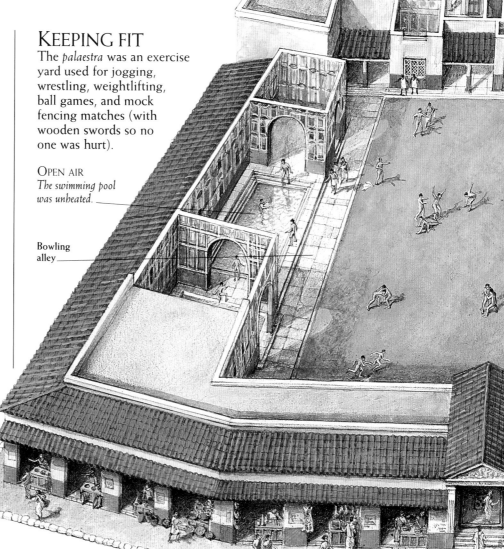

TOILETS
The bath even had its own public toilet.

Carrying handle

Stoppered flask containing oil

Metal skin scraper, known as a strigil

Scraped clean
The Romans had no soap. To clean themselves, they rubbed their bodies with oil, then used a long, thin metal tool, called a strigil, to scrape it off, along with the grime and dirt.

KEEPING FIT
The *palaestra* was an exercise yard used for jogging, wrestling, weightlifting, ball games, and mock fencing matches (with wooden swords so no one was hurt).

OPEN AIR
The swimming pool was unheated.

Bowling alley

FACT file

• There were three baths in Pompeii at the time of the eruption. In Rome there were around 170.

• As businessmen finished work early, they bathed in the middle of the morning, when the water was hottest. Traders and shopkeepers followed in the early afternoon. Most baths closed at sunset.

MEETING AT THE BATHS

Caecilius the banker often went to the baths to meet up with his friends. They left their clothes in the *apodyterium* (changing room), then went to the *tepidarium* (warm room) to relax and acclimatise their bodies to the heat. Next they moved on to the *caldarium* (hot room). Before leaving, Caecilius and his friends would cool off with a refreshing dip in the *frigidarium* (cold pool).

WOMEN ONLY
Women had their own rooms, as mixed bathing was not allowed.

Hot air

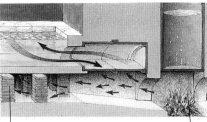

The heating system

The Romans invented a highly efficient system for heating their baths, known as the hypocaust. A central furnace heated the water as well as creating hot air, which circulated under the floors and through hollow tiles on the walls.

The floor was raised on pillars of tiles so that hot air could flow under it.

A fire heated the baths and water in a tank.

COLD ROOM

When Caecilius plunged into the pool, the cold water took his breath away. Other people did not get in the pool, but had cold water poured over them.

WARM ROOM

Caecilius and his friends would lie on marble slabs, while African slaves rubbed oils into their bodies and scraped them clean with strigils.

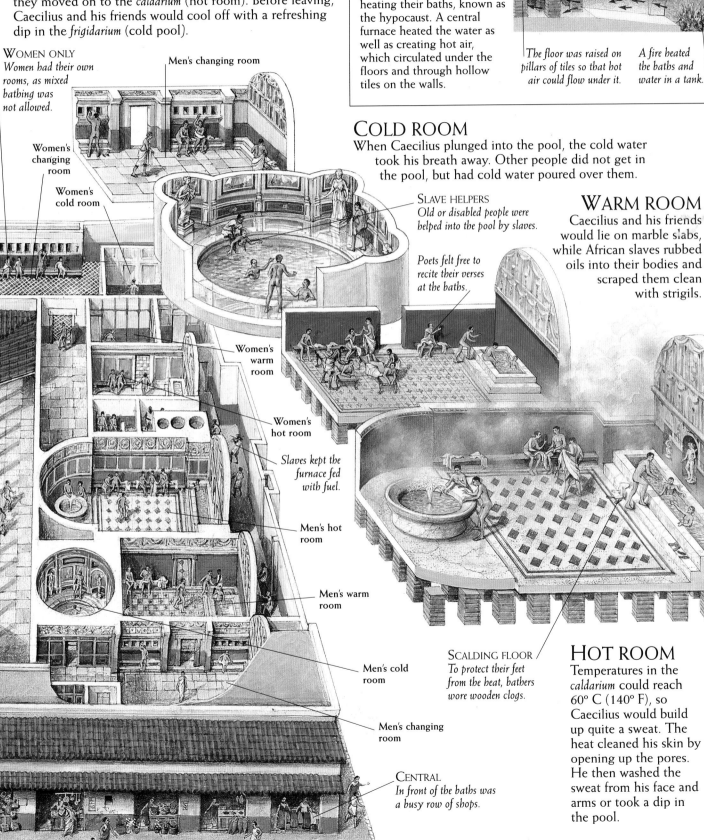

Men's changing room

Women's changing room

Women's cold room

SLAVE HELPERS
Old or disabled people were helped into the pool by slaves.

Poets felt free to recite their verses at the baths.

Women's warm room

Women's hot room

Slaves kept the furnace fed with fuel.

Men's hot room

Men's warm room

Men's cold room

Men's changing room

SCALDING FLOOR
To protect their feet from the heat, bathers wore wooden clogs.

CENTRAL
In front of the baths was a busy row of shops.

HOT ROOM

Temperatures in the *caldarium* could reach 60° C (140° F), so Caecilius would build up quite a sweat. The heat cleaned his skin by opening up the pores. He then washed the sweat from his face and arms or took a dip in the pool.

AT THE THEATRE

THE PEOPLE OF POMPEII LOVED TO SPEND an afternoon at the theatre. One of their favourite plays was *The Haunted House* by Plautus, a comedy with plenty of jokes and funny situations. The theatre only opened during festivals, each lasting three or four days. Audiences could see all kinds of performances, from tragedies to rude farces. The most popular shows were pantomimes, in which an actor danced and mimed a story from Greek legend to the accompaniment of music and song.

Masks
Actors wore masks to represent different types of character. There was a mask for the handsome lover, the young heroine, the foolish old man, the slave, and so on. Comic characters would have huge, grinning mouths.

Timeless tales
Roman authors chose well-known Greek stories for their plays. Some tales, like the story of Hercules, are still enjoyed and have been retold in several films and a cartoon.

Music and song

Musical accompaniment
The Romans liked their plays to be accompanied by music. Songs, dances, and incidental music were often written specially for a performance but, unfortunately, we don't know exactly how they would have sounded.

Bronze cymbals

Apollo, the god of music, with his lyre

Bronze flute

IN THE SHADE
Temperatures in the theatre often reached 40° C (104° F) in summer. To protect the audience from sunstroke, an immense canvas awning (roof) was hoisted over the auditorium. Sailors from Naples were hired to perform this demanding task.

LATECOMER
Modestus had to stand at the back of the auditorium. He was unable to get away from the bakery until just before the performance started.

SEATING
It was important to arrive early to get a good seat. Some people brought cushions with them to make the stone benches more comfortable to sit on. The more important citizens had tickets made from bone, engraved with animals or fruit, and were shown to the front rows by ushers.

BACKSTAGE

The role of Theopropides, the owner of the haunted house, may have been played by Dion. The actor's mask was made from moulded linen, stiffened with plaster and then painted. It was hot to wear, so he would not put it on until the last minute.

THE AWNING
The canvas awning stretched right over the audience but, in order to show inside the theatre, only a small section of it is shown here.

PATRONAGE
This performance was paid for by the fuller (cloth maker) Vesonius, who was standing for election and hoped to win support.

"When the poet Plautus died, Comedy broke down and cried. Then all the laughter, games and fun And all the boundless, bouncy rhythms wept as one."

An epigram (witty poem) written after the death of Plautus.

Rehearsals in Pompeii
By looking closely at mosaics and paintings, we learn a great deal about Roman theatre. In this mosaic, found in Pompeii, one actor is rehearsing dance steps, while another tries on his costume.

MUSICIANS
Songs were accompanied by pipes, cymbals, and a drum.

SCENERY
Painted scenery was used in much the same way as in the modern theatre.

PROPS
A wooden guard dog was one of the props in The Haunted House.

THE PLOT

In the play *The Haunted House*, Tranio, a slave, tricks his master, Theopropides, into believing his house is haunted so that his son can have a party there. When Theopropides finds out, he threatens to whip Tranio, who jumps onto an altar and claims protection from the gods. But in the end Tranio is forgiven, and the play ends happily.

THE AMPHITHEATRE

THE POMPEIANS WERE A BLOODTHIRSTY lot. When they went to the amphitheatre, they wanted to see people killed. The gladiators who fought there were trained in special schools and lived like soldiers, in barracks. Many of them were slaves, condemned criminals, or prisoners of war; others were volunteers, attracted by the prize money. The show began as the gladiators entered the arena in procession, accompanied by trumpeters, who entertained the crowd throughout the day, whipping them up into a frenzy of enthusiasm.

Cruel sport
Gladiator contests were not the only events held in the amphitheatre. The day's entertainment might end with a bear fight or with lions hunting gazelles in the arena.

THE COMBAT
Crescens, the net fighter, was pitted against Murranus, a heavily armed gladiator. Crescens had no protection – not even a helmet. He relied on his speed and agility to outflank Murranus and trap him with his net.

TACTICS
Crescens lunged at Murranus with his trident, while Murranus defended himself with his shield.

NOISE!
Musicians played in the arena while the crowd chanted.

FLINGING THE NET
Crescens flung his net over his opponent.

CHARON
A slave was dressed as Charon, the mythical ferryman who rowed the dead to the underworld.

SHIN ARMOUR
Murranus wore greaves to protect his shins.

The gladiators

EACH GLADIATOR had his speciality. A Thracian carried a small shield and dagger, a *myrmillo* (named after the fish symbol on his helmet) wore heavy armour, an *equites* fought on horseback, a *bestiarius* grappled with wild animals, and a *retarius* fought with a net.

Thracian

Myrmillo

Equites

Bestiarius

RIVAL FANS
Knife fights were common outside the amphitheatre, as well as in the ring.

THE VICTORY

The victorious Crescens saluted his fans. Later that night, graffiti would appear on walls around the town, praising this great gladiator. Fighting to the death was a matter of honour, but we know that at least one gladiator, Polycarpus, "ran away from his opponent in a shameful fashion".

FANS
Female admirers cheered for Crescens.

Riot!
In AD 59, there was a riot in the amphitheatre. Fans from the nearby city of Nuceria shouted abuse at the Pompeians, who retaliated by throwing stones. Fighting broke out and fans from both sides were killed. The incident was reported to Rome, and the amphitheatre was closed down for ten years.

NO MERCY
By pointing their thumbs downwards, fans would have signaled that they wanted Murranus to die.

KILLER BLOW
Charon held a wooden mallet, which may have been used to finish off the defeated gladiator.

DEFEAT
A slave dragged the loser's body from the ring.

CLEAN-UP
The floor of the amphitheatre was covered in sand, which could be swept away easily if it became too bloody.

VESUVIUS AD 79

VESUVIUS HAD BEEN dormant for over 800 years, when pressure building up beneath the volcano caused it to explode in AD 79. At first it was thought that Pompeii had been buried under falling ash and pumice. Now experts believe that the people were killed by fast-moving waves of burning gas and ash called pyroclastic flows, similar to those seen when Mount St Helens erupted in 1980.

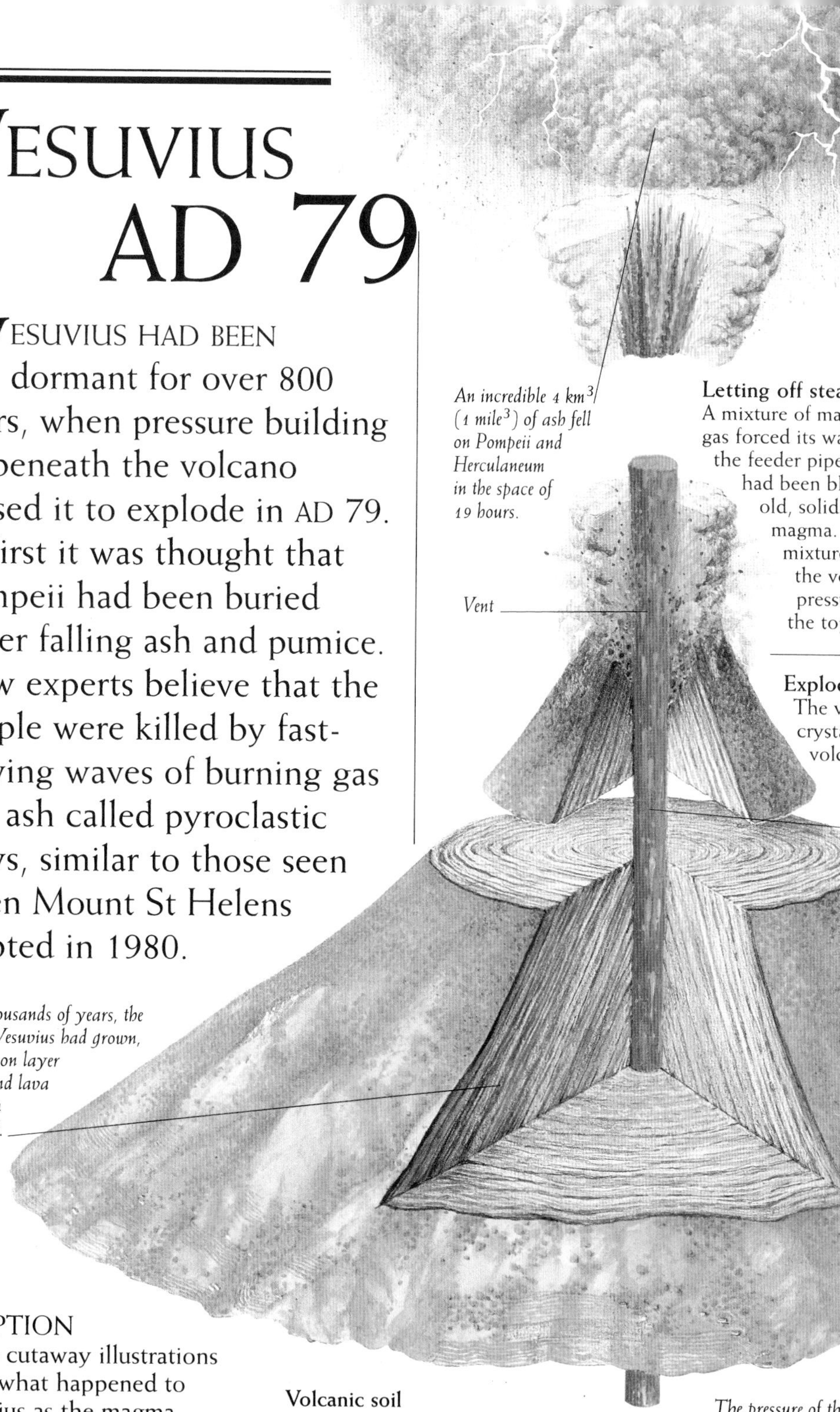

An incredible 4 km³ (1 mile³) of ash fell on Pompeii and Herculaneum in the space of 19 hours.

Vent

Letting off steam
A mixture of magma and gas forced its way through the feeder pipe, which had been blocked by old, solidified magma. When the mixture reached the vent, the pressure blew the top off.

Lightning bolts
The cloud of ash became so dense that it blotted out the sun, turning day into night. Dust particles charged the air with static electricity, causing lightning flashes, which were the only source of light.

Exploded material
The volcano threw out a huge cloud of magma crystals, lapilli (little stones), lumps of pumice, volcanic bombs, and dust particles. Scientists call this material pyroclastic (meaning shattered by fire).

Feeder pipe

Magma

Over thousands of years, the cone of Vesuvius had grown, as layer on layer of ash and lava settled on its slopes.

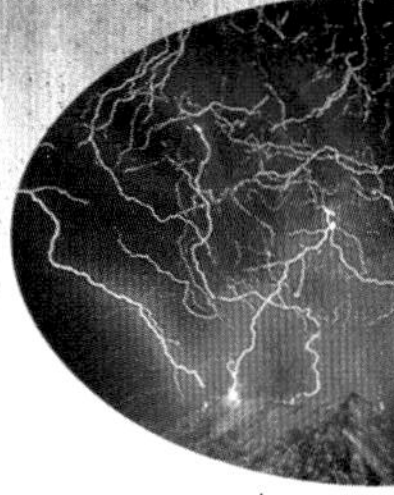

ERUPTION
These cutaway illustrations show what happened to Vesuvius as the magma collected in the huge reservoir, or chamber, 3 km (1.8 miles) underground. The pressure of the accumulating gases on the magma became so intense that it was forced through the feeder pipe, and blasted into fragments high above the mountain.

Volcanic soil
The debris from Vesuvius was rich in minerals and fertilised the soil. Plants would soon grow again on the slopes.

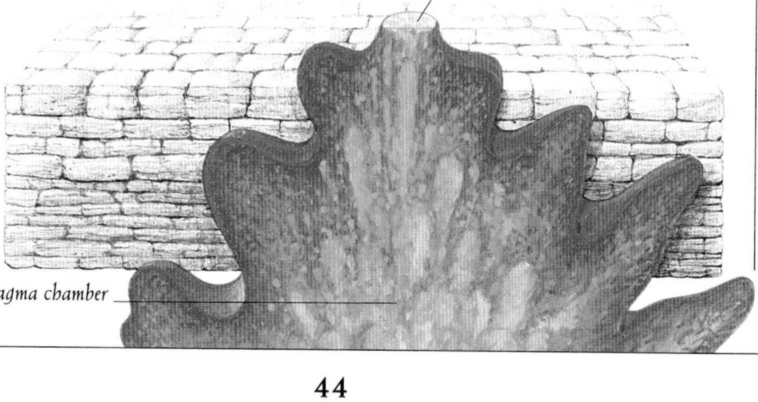

The pressure of the magma built up as it was forced into the narrow feeder pipe.

The magma chamber
The huge chamber filled with magma extended for 10 km (6 miles) beneath the volcano.

Magma chamber

A Plinian eruption
An explosion of ash clouds (shown above to scale) is known as a Plinian eruption, after Pliny – the first person to describe one.

A MODERN-DAY VESUVIUS
When Mount St Helens erupted in the USA on 18 May 1980, photographer Gary Rosenquist was at the scene. He witnessed both the explosion and the pyroclastic flow, which destroyed everything in its path.

After thirty-eight seconds
The original explosion at 8.32 am completely shattered the north face of the mountain. This picture, taken 38 seconds later, shows a cloud of ash rising from the summit as an avalanche of rock roars down the slopes.

... four seconds later ...
The avalanche of old rock is overtaken by a faster-moving surge of newly erupted material. This pyroclastic flow was travelling at speeds of up to 1,000 kph (600 mph).

TREES AFTER THE ERUPTION OF MOUNT ST HELENS

Complete destruction
This photograph shows some of the devastation caused by a volcano. The pyroclastic flow from Mount St Helens caused terrible destruction, uprooting forests and leaving only charred and flattened remains on the hillside.

Run for your life
Rosenquist took this final photograph before racing to his car. As he drove away, marble-sized mud balls were already pounding on his windscreen. Within minutes, it was completely dark and, blindly, he made his way to safety.

... eleven seconds later
The cloud of ash has completely enveloped the avalanche. On the right of the photograph, huge chunks of airborne rock, called lava bombs, are catapulted from the cloud by the force of successive explosions.

Events at Vesuvius in AD 79

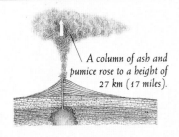

A column of ash and pumice rose to a height of 27 km (17 miles).

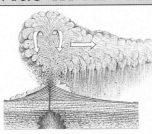

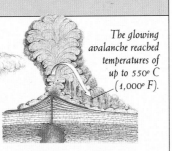

The glowing avalanche reached temperatures of up to 550° C (1,000° F).

1 At midday, an explosion louder than a sonic boom was followed by a burst of gas and magma from the vent in the mountain.

2 Winds blew the volcanic cloud to the southeast. For 19 hours, pumice and ash rained down on Pompeii and the surrounding countryside.

3 The column collapsed at 11.30 pm and a pyroclastic flow destroyed Herculaneum. Pompeii was engulfed by a flow around 7:30 am on 25 August.

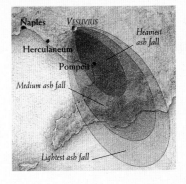

Naples · VESUVIUS · Heaviest ash fall
Herculaneum
Pompeii
Medium ash fall
Lightest ash fall

Deadly breeze
A northwesterly wind carried the fallout of ash 100 km (62 miles) across the Bay of Naples and into southern Italy.

WHAT IS A VOLCANO?

A VOLCANO IS AN OPENING in the Earth's surface. Volcanoes erupt when masses of seething gases and molten rocks (called magma) rise upwards from the Earth's mantle through the crust. Intense pressure forces the gases and magma through the opening, where they explode into the air as clouds of ash and rock particles or as rivers of fiery lava.

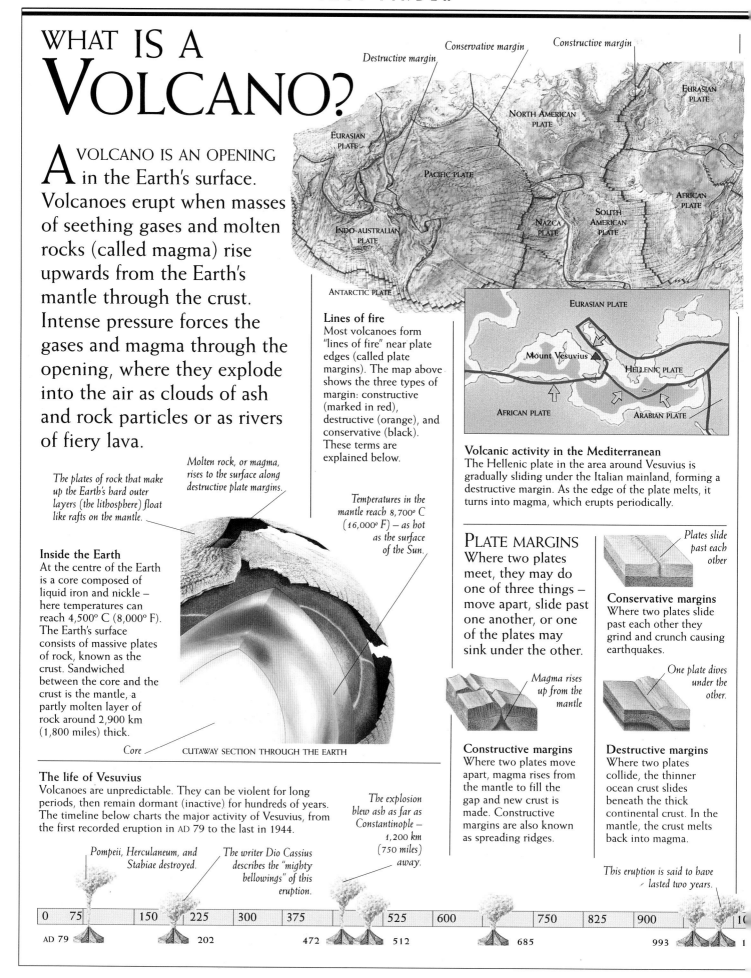

Destructive margin

Conservative margin

Constructive margin

EURASIAN PLATE

NORTH AMERICAN PLATE

EURASIAN PLATE

PACIFIC PLATE

AFRICAN PLATE

INDO-AUSTRALIAN PLATE

NAZCA PLATE

SOUTH AMERICAN PLATE

ANTARCTIC PLATE

Lines of fire
Most volcanoes form "lines of fire" near plate edges (called plate margins). The map above shows the three types of margin: constructive (marked in red), destructive (orange), and conservative (black). These terms are explained below.

EURASIAN PLATE

Mount Vesuvius

HELLENIC PLATE

AFRICAN PLATE

ARABIAN PLATE

Volcanic activity in the Mediterranean
The Hellenic plate in the area around Vesuvius is gradually sliding under the Italian mainland, forming a destructive margin. As the edge of the plate melts, it turns into magma, which erupts periodically.

The plates of rock that make up the Earth's hard outer layers (the lithosphere) float like rafts on the mantle.

Molten rock, or magma, rises to the surface along destructive plate margins.

Temperatures in the mantle reach 8,700° C (16,000° F) – as hot as the surface of the Sun.

Inside the Earth
At the centre of the Earth is a core composed of liquid iron and nickle – here temperatures can reach 4,500° C (8,000° F). The Earth's surface consists of massive plates of rock, known as the crust. Sandwiched between the core and the crust is the mantle, a partly molten layer of rock around 2,900 km (1,800 miles) thick.

Core

CUTAWAY SECTION THROUGH THE EARTH

PLATE MARGINS
Where two plates meet, they may do one of three things – move apart, slide past one another, or one of the plates may sink under the other.

Plates slide past each other

Conservative margins
Where two plates slide past each other they grind and crunch causing earthquakes.

Magma rises up from the mantle

One plate dives under the other.

Constructive margins
Where two plates move apart, magma rises from the mantle to fill the gap and new crust is made. Constructive margins are also known as spreading ridges.

Destructive margins
Where two plates collide, the thinner ocean crust slides beneath the thick continental crust. In the mantle, the crust melts back into magma.

The life of Vesuvius
Volcanoes are unpredictable. They can be violent for long periods, then remain dormant (inactive) for hundreds of years. The timeline below charts the major activity of Vesuvius, from the first recorded eruption in AD 79 to the last in 1944.

The explosion blew ash as far as Constantinople – 1,200 km (750 miles) away.

Pompeii, Herculaneum, and Stabiae destroyed.

The writer Dio Cassius describes the "mighty bellowings" of this eruption.

This eruption is said to have lasted two years.

0	75	150	225	300	375	525	600	750	825	900	10

AD 79   202   472   512   685   993

Temperatures in the ash cloud were measured at 315° C (600° F).

MOUNT ST HELENS, USA, 1980

Red-hot streams of runny lava

MAUNA LAO, HAWAII

Types of eruption
There are two main types of volcanic eruption. Explosive eruptions may happen suddenly, hurling out massive clouds of gas and ash. Basalt lava volcanoes, named after the dark-coloured rock formed as the lava cools, erupt quietly, emitting streams of runny lava. Like many volcanoes, Vesuvius has behaved in both ways.

Natural disaster
PEOPLE LIVING IN THE SHADOW of a volcano know of the dangers, but scientists still cannot predict exactly when a volcano will erupt or what damage it will cause.

Ash and dust
Clouds of ash and dust can suffocate animals, destroy crops, and make transport in the stricken areas difficult.

PINATUBO, PHILIPPINES, 1991

Vulcanologists
A scientist who observes, records, and interprets volcanic activity is called a vulcanologist. Collecting samples of gas and lava from a crater is dangerous work but may help to prevent loss of life in the future.

KILAUEA, HAWAII, 1987

MAYON, PHILIPPINES, 1993

Lava flow
Lava moves slowly and rarely kills people, but it will swallow up trees, roads, houses, and everything else in its path.

Mud flow
Travelling at up to 100 kph (60 mph), a mud flow can wipe out a town in minutes. The avalanche – of rock and volcanic debris as well as mud – can bury people alive. When it dries, it sets as hard as concrete.

WORK AT VESUVIUS
The first vulcanological observatory was built at Vesuvius in 1841. Many important vulcanologists worked there, including Luigi Palmieri, the inventor of the seismograph, and Giuseppe Mercalli, who devised a scale for measuring the intensity of earthquakes.

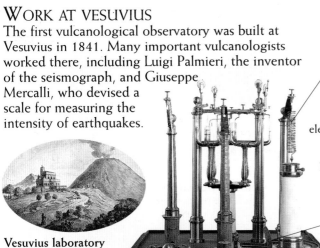

Vesuvius laboratory
The observatory was set up so that scientists could measure volcanic activity.

Delicate spring devices detected even the faintest tremor.

Palmieri's seismograph
The seismograph was the first electronic instrument to measure ground tremors. Palmieri hoped he might be able to predict an eruption.

The magnitude of the tremors was recorded here.

From 1751, early excavations around Pompeii were regularly halted by volcanic activity.

A volcanic bomb of several tons was found in a garden 5 km (3 miles) from the crater.

VESUVIUS TODAY

Future activity
Vesuvius today looks harmless, but it will almost certainly erupt again. Scientists at the Vesuvius Observatory have installed measuring equipment in the area and, by analysing this data, hope to be able to predict future activity.

After this eruption, Vesuvius seemed dormant. Land was cultivated right up to the crater.

More than 4,000 people perished in the worst eruption since AD 79.

| 25 | 1200 | 1275 | 1350 | 1425 | 1500 | 1575 | 1650 | 1725 | 1875 | 1950 |

1500   1631   1682   1822

The last eruption to date was in 1944.

Index

Acknowledgments

Dorling Kindersley would like to thank: Robert Graham and Angela Koo for research; Venice Shone and Peter Radcliffe for design; Mary Atkinson for editorial help; Chris Bernstein for the index.

Picture credits
c=centre; t=top; b=bottom; l=left; r=right; a=above

The Ancient, Art and Architecture Collection: Ronald Sheridan 19tr; Archivi Alinari: 32tl; AKG, London: 8c (below); 9cr, 14b; Erich Lessing 15br; Museo Archeologico di Napoli: 2cr, 27t, 28bl, 29br, 34bl; The Bridgeman Art Library: Museo Archeologico Nazionale, Naples: *The Baker and his Wife* (c.50 AD) 20tl; *A Fight in the Amphitheatre* (1st century AD) 43 tr; Musée des Beaux-Arts, Lille/Giraudon: *Vulcan's Forge*, Flemish School, (15th century) 18tl; Museo e Gallerie Nazionali di Capodimonte, Naples: *Death of Julius Caesar*, Vincenzo Camuccini (1773-1844) 9cb; *Gold Bulla from the House of the Menander*, (79AD) 14cla; **British Museum:** 6bl, 9br, 11cr, 15bl, 18bl, 33tl, 38cl; **Camerapress:** Grazia Neri 31tr; **Colorific:** Gary Braasch/Woodfin Camp 45tr; **Corbis:** Roger Ressmeyer 11tr; **G. Dagli Orti:** 33tr; **Jean Dieuzaide:** Musée des Augustins, Toulouse: *L'éruption du Vésuve et la Mort de Pline*, Pierre Henri de Valenciennes (1813)16/17c; **CM Dixon:** 5cr, 8cr (below); 14tl, 22tr, 34/35b; **Mary Evans Picture Library:** 8bl, 9bc/cl (below), 16cla, 26/27c, 29tl; **Lin Esposito:** 28bc, 29ca; **Fine Art Photographs:** 6/7c; **The Ronald Grant Archive:** *Asterix Conquers America* © 20th Century Fox/Gaumont 9cl; *Hercules Unchained* © Warner-Pathé (1958) 40cl; **Sonia Halliday Photographs:** 8br; **Robert Harding Picture Library:** 8tl, 9bl, 10bl, 15car, 28br, 30c, 41cr; **Frank Lane Picture Agency:** A.Nardi/Panda Photo 47 cr (below); **National Geographic Society:** O.Louis Mazzatenta 29tr; **The National Trust Photographic Library:** *Pompeii* by Jacob Philipp Hackert (1737-1809), John Hammond 28tl; **Planet Earth Pictures:** Bourseiller and Durieux 19br, 47tl/ca; Krafft 47tr/c; **Phototeque des Musées de la Ville de Paris:** *The Pompeian Forum: a general plan*, Léon Jaussely (1910)12/13b; **Rex Features:** Sipa-Press 47cr; Sipa-Press/T.Nishiinoue 44tr; **Photo RMN:** Chuzeville 14c; **Gary Rosenquist:** 45tl/ca/cl/cr; **Scala:** 36tl; Musei Capitolini, Roma 40tl; Museo Nazionale, Napoli 10tl, 37t; Palazzo Madama, Roma 8c; **Science Photo Library:** Peter Menzel 19cr; **Frank Spooner Pictures:** Morrison/Liaison 47cl; **University of Bradford / Department of Archaeological Sciences:** Rick Jones 30tl; **Roger - Viollet:** 30bl; **Visual Arts Library:** Artephot/ M.E. Boucher 13cra; Artephot/Held 11c (below); Nimatallah 8cl (below); **Werner Forman Archive:** 28cr, 33br; Museo Archeologico Nazionale, Naples 15tl, 33ca: Museo Capitoline, Rome 40bl.

Jacket: **Bruce Coleman Collection:** Stefano Amantini front cover cra.